Collins Primary Science

MOVING THINGS

Linda Howe

Resources Needed

Collections To Be Made

Things with moving parts (2)

Different kinds of packaging (3)

Cylinders of different types (4, 14)

Rolling objects (5, 8)

Different types of paper (7, 10)

General Resources

Paper (1, 9, 13)

Pencils (1)

Building blocks (3, 14)

Card (3, 4, 9)

Sticky tape (3, 10, 11)

Cardboard tubes (4)

String (5, 6, 9)

Chalk (5, 7)

Strips of different textured materials (5)

Balloons (6)

Balloon pump (6)

Paper plates (6, 9)

A4 paper (7)

Thick card/plank of wood (8)

Polystyrene trays (9)

Short garden canes (10)

Lengths of wire (10)

Small beads (10, 12)

Scissors (11)

Glue (11)

Food colouring (12)

Glitter (12)

Plastic bottles (12)

Soil (13)

Sand (13, 14)

Sweet jar/plastic aquarium (13)

Brick (12, 13)

Pole (14)

Other Resources

Bicycle pump/battery fan (6)

Cooking oil (12)

Coloured aquarium gravel (12)

Contents

	Resources needed	2
1	How do we move?	4
2	How do things move?	6
3	Rolling things	8
4	Which things roll furthest?	10
5	Moving on different surfaces	12
6	Balloons	14
7	Moving air	16
8	Rolling down slopes	18
9	Kites	20
10	Windmills	22
11	Paper aeroplanes	24
12	Moving colours	26
13	Moving creatures	28
14	Moving heavy loads	30
	Acknowledgements	32

1   HOW DO WE MOVE?

Think about young babies. Make a list of things that you can do but a baby cannot do.
Can a baby talk, walk, feed itself, swim, ride a bicycle, run, jump or hop? Can you think of anything else?

Draw some pictures of some things that you like doing. You could draw a red ring around things that you do on your own and a blue ring around things that you do with friends. Put a cross next to those activities for which you need something to help; like a ball, bike or skipping rope.

Which things can you do indoors and which can you do outdoors?

How can you move?

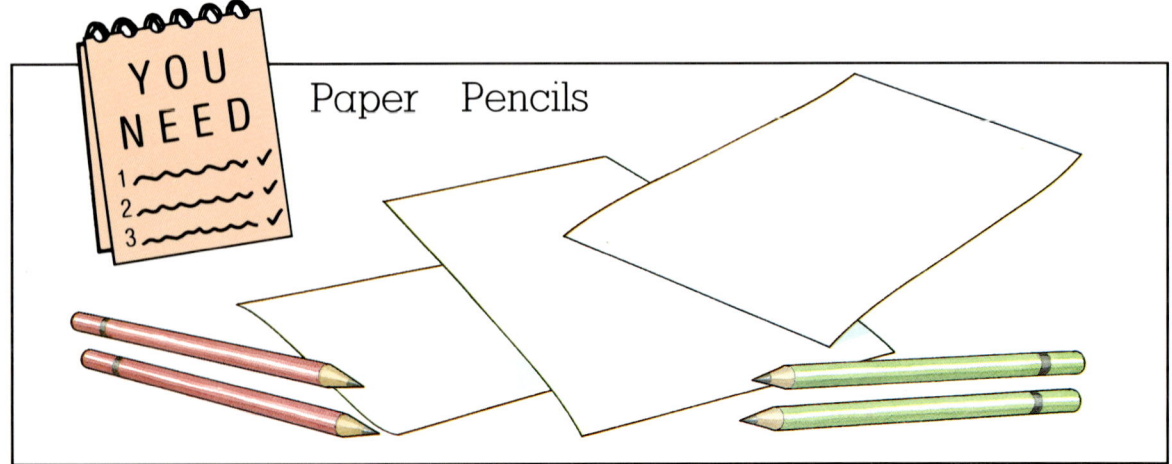

YOU NEED   Paper   Pencils

ACTIVITY
- A -

Draw a picture of yourself and label the different parts of your body. Mark a cross everywhere where your body can turn. Can you name these parts? Can you say which parts of your body can turn many ways, like your wrist, and which can only move one way, like your elbow?

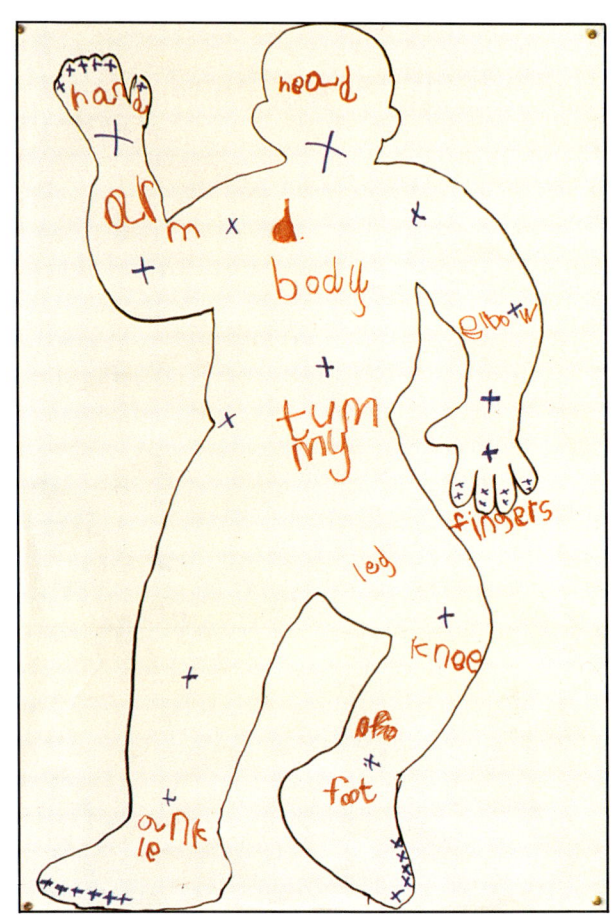

ACTIVITY
- B -

Work with a friend. Can you do some things for your friend to copy? You could try jumping, hopping, standing on one leg, shaking your head as well as your own ideas. When you have had a turn change places with your friend and copy what they do. Which things do you find hard to do and which do you find easy?

Draw some picture instructions for a friend to copy.

2 HOW DO THINGS MOVE?

How many moving things can you find in school?
Start with the doors and windows.
Do they open in or out?
Can you make some push and pull signs?
You could stick them on the doors around the school.

Are there any curtains or blinds in the school?
Can you see how they move?
Do they go up and down or from side to side?

Which parts of the taps move?
Do they all turn the same way for on and off?

How do the lights turn on?
Do they have a pull switch, a push switch or a turn switch?
Can you find any other switches?
You might find switches on heaters, televisions, and videos as well as other things.

What other moving things can you find?

How do things move?

Choose one of the objects to look at closely. Can you see which parts move? Do they move up and down or round and round? Is there just one moving part or do many parts move? Choose another thing. Does it move in the same way as the first object? How is it different? Are the moving parts round or long or another shape? Look closely at the other things. How do they move? Why do they have moving parts?

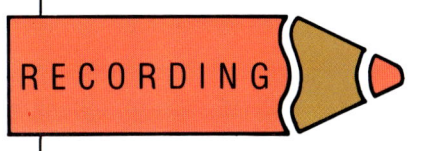

Draw some objects. Look at them closely to make sure that you draw each part carefully.
Find some other things with moving parts to draw. The inside of a clock is a good example.

3 ROLLING THINGS

How many ways do different creatures move?
Which birds can;
fly?   swim?   hop?   walk?   climb?

How do these creatures move?

fish

cats

kangaroos

seals

snakes

Draw some pictures. Can you draw creatures that can fly, hop, jump, swim, slither and swim?

Can you find out which things roll?

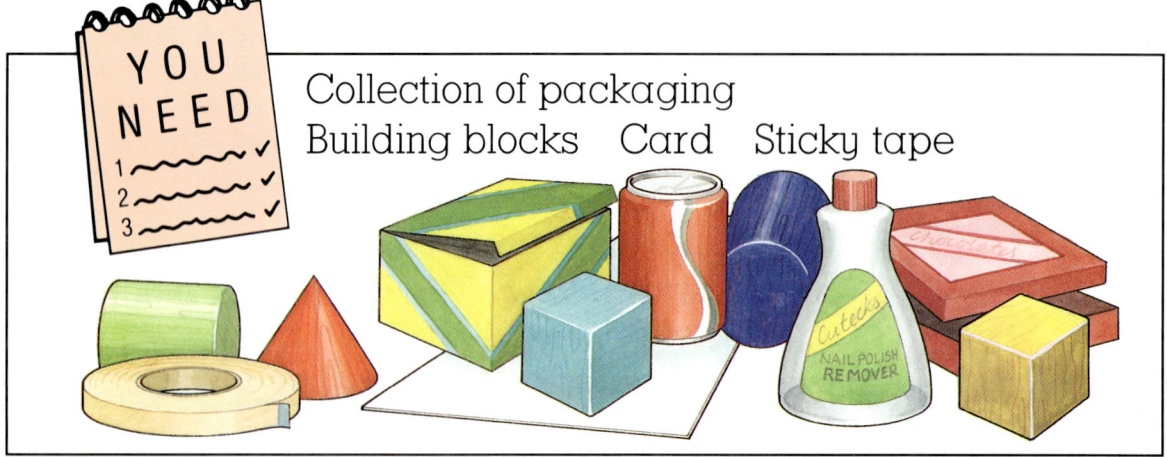

YOU NEED
Collection of packaging
Building blocks   Card   Sticky tape

Try out your packaging. Can you make a set of rolling and non-rolling things? Which sorts of shapes move? Do they have flat or curved sides?

ACTIVITY -B-

Take the building blocks.
Can you sort out the things that you think will roll? Try them.
Did you have things in the right sets?
Which sorts of shapes were in the roll set?

ACTIVITY -C-

Make some card shapes. Fix them together with sticky tape. Which ones do you think will roll? Try them out. Did you choose the right ones?

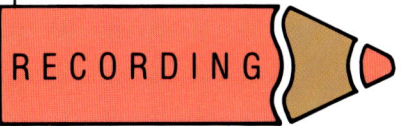

Stick the packaging and your card shapes into rolling and non-rolling sets using strong glue and thick card.

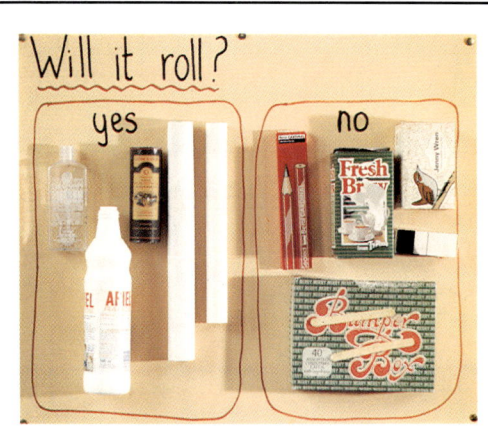

4 WHICH THINGS ROLL FURTHEST?

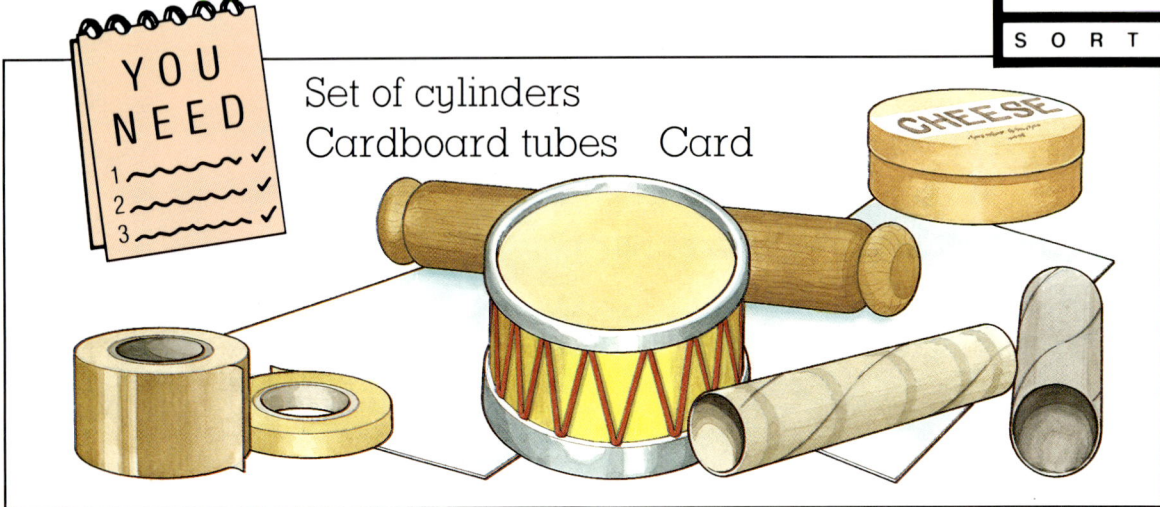

YOU NEED
Set of cylinders
Cardboard tubes   Card

Choose a cylinder. Starting off from a line on the floor take turns in rolling your cylinders. Which things roll:
- in a straight line?
- in a curved line?
- smoothly?
- with a wobble?

Which things roll furthest? Are they heavy or light, fat or thin?

Can you make some sets?
You could try:
- things that roll in straight and curved lines
- things that roll smoothly and with a wobble
- things that roll a long way and not very far
and your own ideas

Make sets of cylinders to show how they rolled. Try:
- rolled straight/curved
- rolled far/not far
- rolled smoothly/with a wobble.

ACTIVITY -B-

Work in a group. Everyone should have a cardboard tube.
Choose a shape to cut from a piece of card. Everyone in your group should choose a different shape.
Cut out two identical shapes and stick one on each end of the cardboard tube.
Try rolling the tubes in turn.
Which ones will roll and which will not roll?
If you have a shape that will roll can you stop it rolling?
If you have a shape that will not roll can you make it roll?

You could try sticking a new shape over the ends of your tube or cutting your shape to change it.
What else could you try?
Try again.
Which ones roll now? Which ones will not roll?

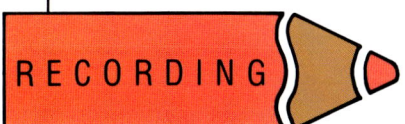

RECORDING

Draw your shape on a chart. Record whether your first shape rolled and draw the shape you changed it to.

11

5 MOVING ON DIFFERENT SURFACES

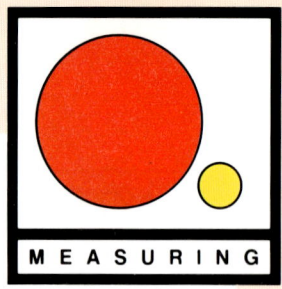

Think about things that move along roads. Some have four wheels like cars, lorries, vans, buses and tractors.
Can you think of any others?

Some vehicles have more than four wheels.
Can you find pictures of any?

Bicycles, motorbikes, mopeds and scooters only have two wheels. A tricycle has three wheels.
Can you think of any other vehicle with three wheels?

Draw some pictures of things that travel on roads. Draw things with two, three, four or more wheels.

How far do things travel on different surfaces?

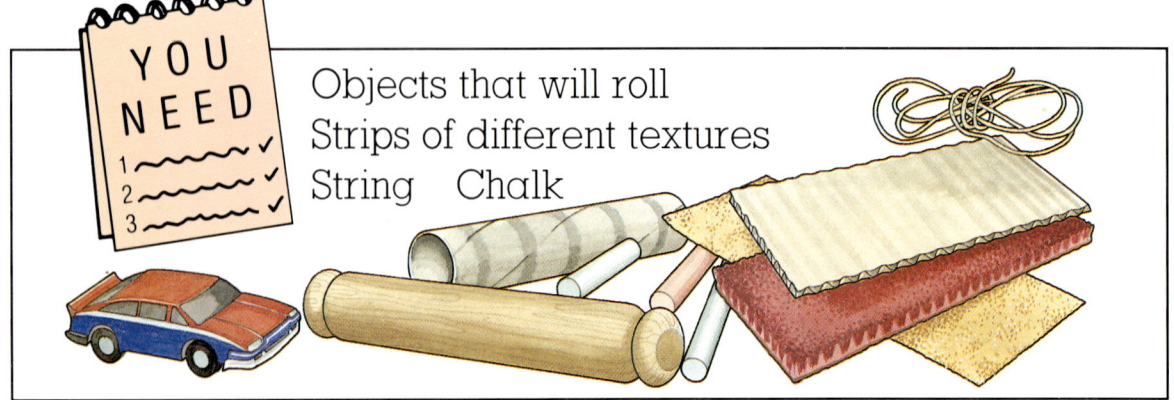

YOU NEED
Objects that will roll
Strips of different textures
String   Chalk

12

ACTIVITY -A-

Make a chalk line on the floor.
Choose an object which rolls well.
Start it on the line and give it a push.
How far did it travel? How will you measure?
You could cut a piece of string from the line to where the roller stopped or measure with your feet.
You could also try your own ideas for measuring.

ACTIVITY -B-

Try putting a strip of a different texture on the floor, beginning at the chalk line.
Starting the roller at the line, give it a push.
Does the roller travel as far as it did before?
Measure again and try some other surfaces.
Which surface does it roll best on?

RECORDING

Make a chart to record the measurements. You might want to stick your pieces of string on the chart.

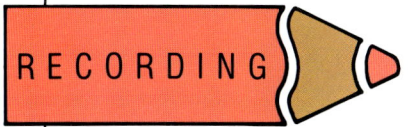

BALLOONS

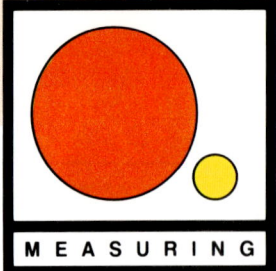

How a balloon moves

YOU NEED: Balloons, Balloon pump, String, Paper plates, Bicycle pumps and/or battery fans

Measure round a balloon before it is blown up, using a piece of string.
Cut the string to size.
Give the balloon five pumps using the balloon pump and measure it again with string.
Now pump the balloon up until it is fully blown, stopping after every five pumps to measure and cut the string.

Can you say how many pumps it took altogether to blow up the balloon fully?
What can you notice about your pieces of string?
Do they get longer or shorter?
How much longer is the last piece than the first?

Try this with a different shape of balloon.
Does the same thing happen?
What do you think makes the balloon grow?

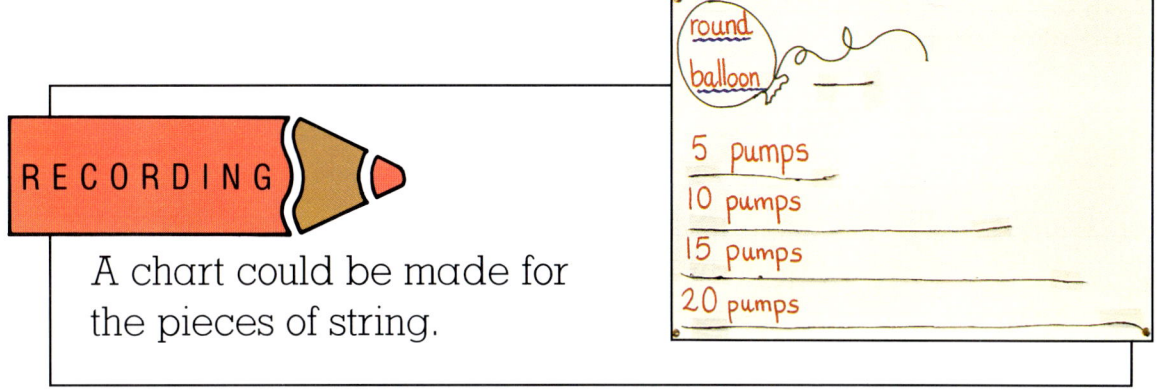

RECORDING

A chart could be made for the pieces of string.

Make a start line and a finish line on the floor.
How many different ways can you get a
balloon from the start to the finish?
You could try:
- carrying it
- kicking it
- putting it between your knees and jumping
- blowing it
- rolling it
- blowing it with a pump or a fan
- flapping a paper plate behind it

as well as ideas of your own.

Can you find the quickest way? You could count how many seconds it takes to get the balloon from one line to the other. Which way is the slowest way of moving the balloon?

RECORDING

You could record what you did and the number of seconds it took for the balloon to move from start to finish.

7 MOVING AIR

Have you been out on a windy day?
What sort of things get blown about?
You might feel the wind blow your hair, clothes and body.
Sometimes it is hard to walk in a strong wind.

Imagine that you are out in a very strong wind. Can you feel it blowing you?
You have to get to a friend's house. How will you get there?
What can you do to help yourself walk in the wind?
You might see trees moving, leaves swirling, litter flying as well as other things.
What else is blowing around?

Make a picture of yourself on a windy day. You could paint yourself and stick on leaves and litter blowing about. Can you think how to show the wind?

Making a wind to move a paper fish

YOU NEED
Different types of paper
Sheets of A4 paper   Chalk

Choose one kind of paper. Cut a large fish out of your paper.
Take a sheet of A4 paper and fold it into a paper fan.
Draw a start and finish line on the floor.
Put the fish on the start line and have a race with your friends to see whose fish can be moved fastest with the paper fans.

Think about what might have made a difference.
It might have been:
- the kinds of paper
- the size of the fish
- the person flapping
- how the fan was used

Can you try some tests to find out?

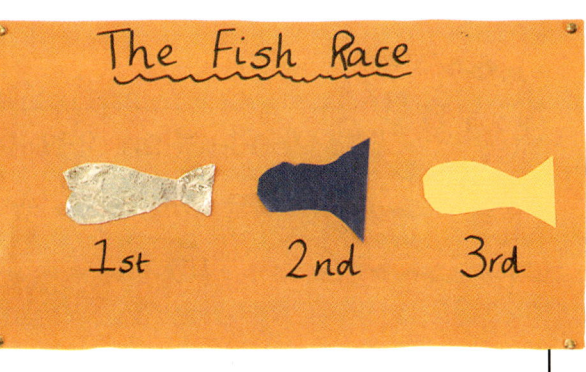

Record the order in which the fish arrived at the finish line either by drawing or sticking the fish on a chart.

17

ROLLING DOWN SLOPES

Jack and Jill
  Went up the hill
To fetch a pail of water;
  Jack fell down
And broke his crown
  And Jill came tumbling after.

Do you think that you could fall up hill?
Is it easiest to walk, run or ride a bike up hill or down hill? Why do you think one way is easiest?

Put a toy car on the floor. Does it move by itself?
Make a hill using wood or card and put the car at the bottom of the hill. Does it move?
Now put the car near the top of the hill. What happens? If you put the car in different places on your hill does the same thing happen?

Which slope makes the roller travel furthest?

YOU NEED   Collection of rollers   Chalk
Sheet of thick card or a plank of wood

Use the card or wood to make a slope.
Can you test to find which roller will travel furthest away from the slope?
Will you start all the rollers in the same place on the slope?
How will you measure how far the rollers travelled?
Try your test. Which roller goes furthest?

Change your slope. You might make it steeper or not as steep. Try your test again. Do the same rollers go furthest?
Try all sorts of different slopes to see whether the same rollers always go furthest.

On a chart draw the slopes and fill in which rollers travel furthest.

KITES

Have you ever seen kites flying on a windy day? Kites have been popular for hundreds of years. In China they have a kite festival. Can you find out about what they do?

Have you ever flown a kite? You have to hold the string tightly or you might lose it.

SOMETHING TO TRY

On a windy day tie a balloon to the end of a piece of string, hold the other end tightly and go outside. Can you feel the wind trying to pull the string out of your hand? Try running with the balloon whilst holding the string tightly. What can you feel? You might want to see what happens if you let go of the balloon. You could tie a message on your balloon before you let go.

Making a kite

YOU NEED

Cardboard   Paper plates   Polystyrene trays
Foil trays   String   Coloured paper

ACTIVITY

To make a kite, choose one of the trays or plates or cut a cardboard shape of your own. Make a hole in one end for the string. Try making a tail with string and coloured paper for the other end. Join a string at one end of the kite and if you have a tail join it at the other.
Try your kite outside.
Does it fly well?
Does it fly as well as your friends' kites?
Can you think of any ways of changing your kite?
You could try:
- a longer or shorter string
- a longer or shorter tail
- adding or removing a tail

What else could you try?
Decorate your kite to make it look bright.

RECORDING

Draw your kite and write the changes you made next to it.

WINDMILLS

Can you think of some things that move in the wind? You might think of:

windmills

weather vanes

flags

yachts

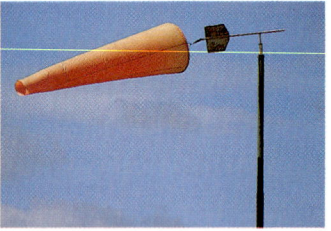
windsocks

Which things blow in the wind and which things turn in the wind?

What can you find out about windmills? You might see pictures of old and new windmills. Windmills might be used for turning stones to grind corn, pumping water or making electricity. Are there any windmills near your school that you could visit?

Making windmills

YOU NEED

Short garden canes   Lengths of wire
Small beads   Different types of paper
Sticky tape

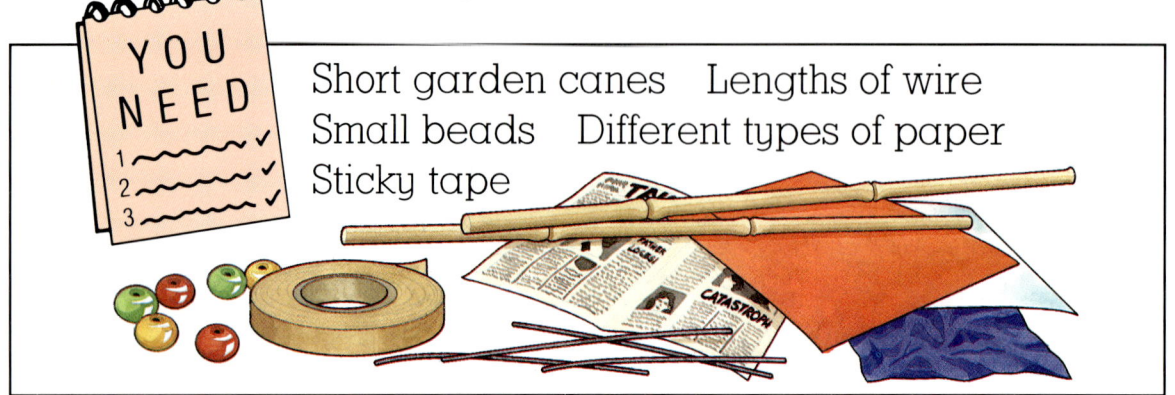

ACTIVITY

Choose one of the kinds of paper.
Try to use a different paper from your friends.
Cut a square of paper and fold it from corner to corner and then again.
Open the paper out and draw a circle in the middle.
Cut along the fold lines as far as the circle and fold every other corner to the middle and glue them together.

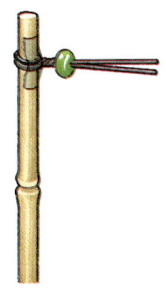

Wrap a piece of wire around the cane and secure it with sticky tape.
Twist the ends of the wire together and pass them through a bead and then through the centre of the folded paper shape.
Add another bead and fold the ends down.

Run holding the cane or blow the windmill and watch what happens. Which type of paper turns best?

RECORDING

Photos could be taken of the windmills. You could tell each other about the paper you used and how well your windmill turned.

23

11 PAPER AEROPLANES

Making a paper aeroplane

YOU NEED: Scrap paper   Scissors   Glue   Sticky tape

 Try making your own paper aeroplanes. You could make one of these types or try an idea of your own.

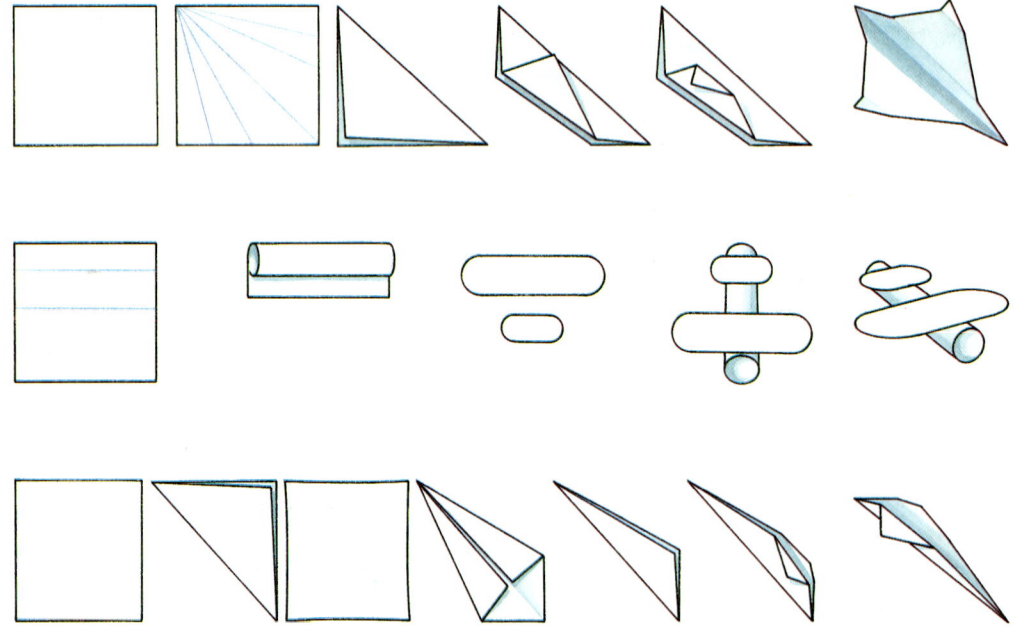

Try several designs and then choose the one which you like best. You might like it because it flies the fastest, straightest, furthest or for some reason of your own.

24

When you find your favourite design try making it in different sizes. Which size do you think is best? Can you improve your aeroplane? You could try putting a paper clip on the nose, bending the wings up, sticking on some flaps as well as other ideas of your own.

When you have an aeroplane that you are happy with, you might like to decorate it and show it to your friends.

Draw some pictures to show someone else how to make your aeroplane. You could also stick the ones you tried out on a chart and say why you did not choose them.

12 MOVING COLOURS

Have you ever seen a funfair at night?
Did you see moving coloured lights? Which colours did you see?
Where else might you see moving coloured lights? You might see:

traffic at night

fireworks

Can you think of anything else?

Using black paper and coloured paint, paint a picture of coloured lights at night.

Have you ever looked through a kaleidoscope?
You might be able to find one to look through.
Can you see changing coloured patterns?
How many colours are used?
How many different patterns can you see?

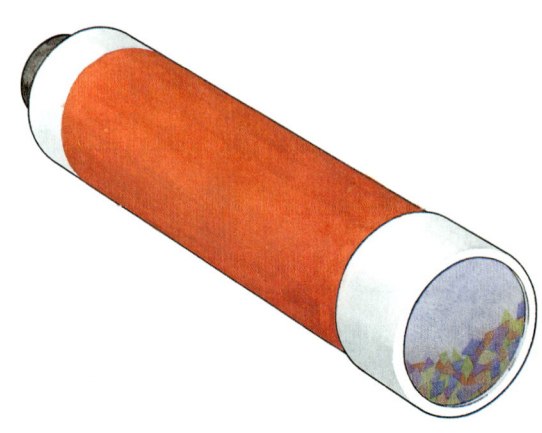

26

Making a coloured roller

Use a bottle to make a roller that will make coloured patterns as it rolls.

You could try:
- Putting mixed coloured beads, glitter, sequins or aquarium gravel in a bottle, putting the top on and rolling it
- Putting coloured water with beads or sequins in a bottle, putting the top on and rolling
- Putting coloured water and cooking oil in a bottle, putting the top on and rolling
- Your own ideas

Which rollers do you think make the best patterns?

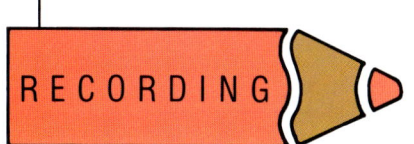 Draw what you put in your bottle.

MOVING CREATURES

Imagine a big, heavy creature moving around. It might be a dinosaur or an elephant. Do you think it would move quickly or slowly? Do you think that it would move quietly or noisily? What sorts of noises might you hear?

Now think about very tiny creatures like ants, ladybirds or tadpoles.
How do they move? Do you think that they move quickly or slowly? Would you hear:
- an ant running across the garden?
- a worm crawling in the soil?
- a spider running across the room?

Can you think of other hard-to-hear noises made by creatures?

How do minibeasts move?

YOU NEED: Piece of old wood or a brick   Soil   Sand   Black paper   Sweet jar or an old aquarium

ACTIVITY -A-

You might find an old rotting tree stump or a block of wood whilst out on a walk or you might leave a piece of old wood or a brick outside for a week. Bring the wood in and put it on a piece of paper or lift the brick and look underneath it.

How many little creatures can you find? You might see:

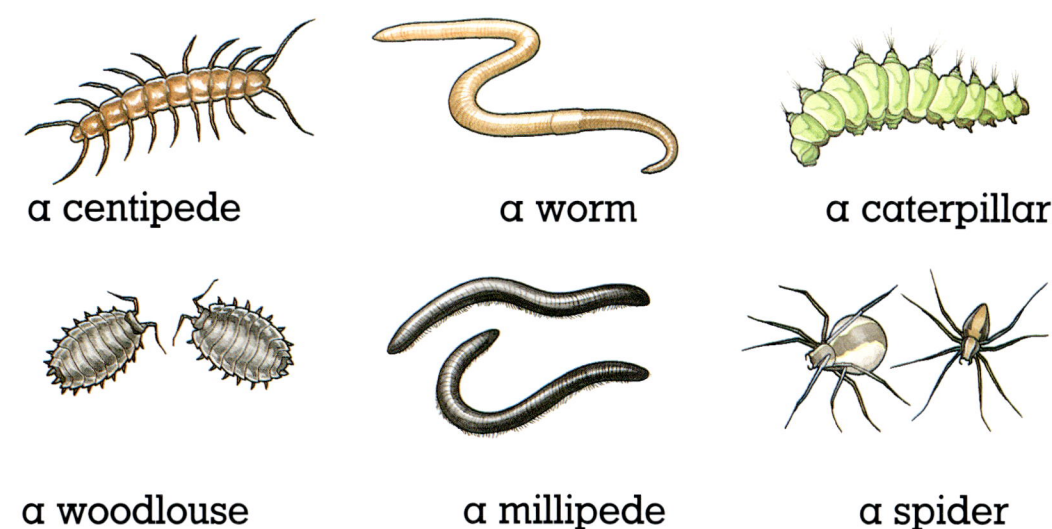

a centipede   a worm   a caterpillar

a woodlouse   a millipede   a spider

and many other minibeasts. Watch each creature move on a piece of paper. Can you see how they move? How many legs do the creatures have?

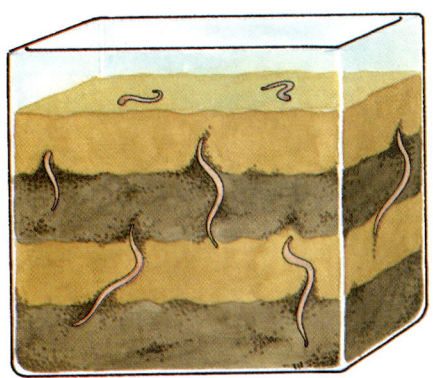

Create a wormery in the classroom. Find some worms. In an aquarium or a plastic sweet jar put a layer of soil followed by a layer of sand. Repeat until the jar is full. Put your worms in the wormery and then wrap black paper around the sides. Remove the paper each day to look at the worms. Can you say what happens to the soil and sand? How do the worms move?

 Look closely at the creatures and make drawings of them.

14 MOVING HEAVY LOADS

How do we move big, heavy loads?

They might travel on a lorry, a train or a barge.

Sometimes tractors or cranes are used to help pull or lift the loads.
Heavy loads are often carried on big ships. Cranes lift the things onto the ships.

Think about the sorts of heavy loads that might be carried. Loads might be cars, sand or gravel, machinery, coal or stone, or bricks. Can you think of some others?

Have you ever tried to carry a heavy load? Can you think of anything which might make it easier to carry? You might use a trolley or ask a friend to help.

Moving or lifting a heavy load

YOU NEED

Brick   Carrier bag full of sand
Toy lorry   Pole   Cylindrical objects
Cuboid blocks

ACTIVITY – A –

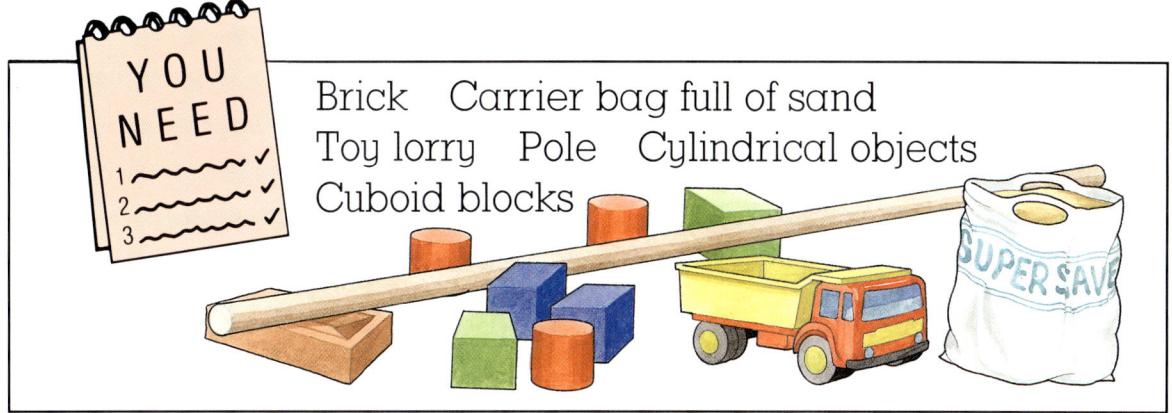

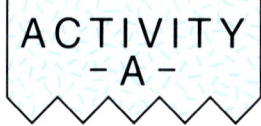

Take the bag of sand and try carrying it by yourself. Now ask a friend to help carry it. Try putting a pole through the handles of the bag and carrying it on your shoulders. Which way of carrying do you think is easiest?

ACTIVITY – B –

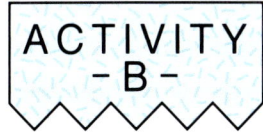

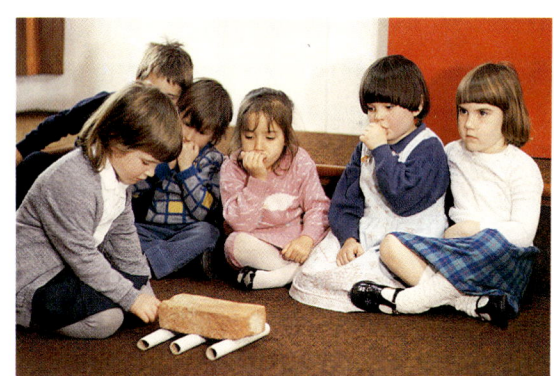

Take a brick, put it on the floor and give it a push. How far does it move?
If you ask your friends to help push how far does it go?
Try putting the brick on a toy lorry and giving it a push. How far does it go? You could also try putting the brick on blocks and pushing it.
Does it go further on cuboid blocks or cylinders? Can you think of other ways to move the brick?

RECORDING

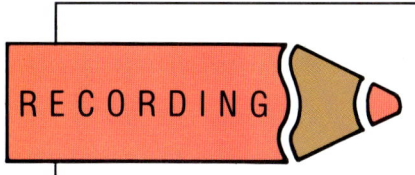

On a chart, show the ways you used to move the lorry and the distance the brick moved each time.

Acknowledgements

Copyright © 1990 Linda Howe
ISBN 0 00 317539 1

Published by Collins Educational London and Glasgow

Design by David Bennett Books Ltd.
Illustrations by Amelia Rosato and Sally Neave
Commissioned photography by Oliver Hatch
Picture Research by Nance Fyson and Gwenan Morgan

Typeset by Kalligraphics Ltd., Horley, Surrey
Printed and bound in Wing King Tong, Hong Kong

All rights reserved. No part of this book may be reproduced or transmitted in any form or by any means, without the prior permission of the publisher.

The publishers thank St. John's First and Middle School, Ealing, London and Woolpit County Primary School, Suffolk for their kind co-operation in the production of Collins Primary Science.

Photographs – The publisher would like to thank the following for permission to reproduce photographs.

Ace Photo Agency 22tr; ANT/NHPA 8br; Ardea London Ltd 8tl, 8tr, 8bc; Douglas Baglin/NHPA 8bl; Barnaby's 26l, 30t, 30c; Bruce Coleman Ltd 22tl; Nance Fyson 12t, 12c, 12b(x2); Robert Harding Picture Library 22bl, 22bc, 22br, 26r, 30b; Daily Telegraph 20

t = top, b = bottom, l = left, r = right, c = centre